W9-DGS-835

What Are
Forests?

by Lisa Trumbauer

Consulting Editor: Gail Saunders-Smith, Ph.D.

Consultant: Sandra Mather, Ph.D., Professor Emerita,
Department of Geology and Astronomy,
West Chester University
West Chester, Pennsylvania

Pebble Books

an imprint of Capstone Press
Mankato, Minnesota

Pebble Books are published by Capstone Press
151 Good Counsel Drive, P.O. Box 669, Mankato, Minnesota 56002
http://www.capstone-press.com

1 2 3 4 5 6 07 06 05 04 03 02

Library of Congress Cataloging-in-Publication Data
Trumbauer, Lisa, 1963–
    What are forests? / by Lisa Trumbauer.
    p. cm.—(Earth features)
    Includes bibliographical references (p. 23) and index.
    ISBN 0-7368-0988-0
    1. Forests and forestry—Juvenile literature. [1. Forests and forestry.] I. Title.
II. Series.
SD376 .T78 2002
333.75—dc21   2001000267

Summary: Simple text and photographs introduce forests and their features.

Note to Parents and Teachers

The Earth Features series supports national science standards for
units on landforms of the earth. The series also supports geography
standards for using maps and other geographic representations.
This book describes and illustrates forests. The photographs
support early readers in understanding the text. The repetition of
words and phrases helps early readers learn new words. This book
also introduces early readers to subject-specific vocabulary words,
which are defined in the Words to Know section. Early readers may
need assistance to read some words and to use the Table of
Contents, Words to Know, Read More, Internet Sites, and
Index/Word List sections of the book.

Table of Contents

4

A forest is a large area
of land covered with trees.

Some forests receive a lot of rain. Some forests receive little rain.

Rain falls almost every day in a tropical rain forest. The rain makes the forest green.

Tropical rain forests grow in places that are warm all year.

Temperate forests grow where winters are cold and summers are warm.

Temperate forests have mostly deciduous trees. Their leaves change color during autumn.

16

Many evergreen forests
grow in places that
are mostly cold.

Evergreen forests have mostly coniferous trees. Their leaves stay green all year. Evergreen leaves are called needles.

Redwood National Park

California

Redwood National Park
is in California.
The tallest trees in
the world grow there.

Words to Know

coniferous—a kind of tree with cones and leaves called needles; needles stay green all year on most evergreen trees; coniferous seeds are found in a cone.

deciduous—a kind of tree that loses its leaves every autumn; the branches are bare during winter; new leaves grow each spring.

evergreen forest—a forest in which most trees are coniferous; evergreen forests cover 2.7 billion acres (1.1 billion hectares) in North America, Europe, and Asia.

temperate forest—a forest in which most trees are deciduous; oak trees, birch trees, and elm trees are common in temperate forests.

tropical rain forest—a forest in the tropics; the tropics is an area near the equator that is hot and rainy; rain falls almost every day in tropical rain forests.

Read More

Fowler, Allan. *Our Living Forests.* Rookie Read-about Science. New York: Children's Press, 1999.

Hall, Cally. *Forests.* Closer Look At. Brookfield, Conn.: Copper Beech Books, 1999.

Morris, Neil. *Forests.* The Wonders of Our World. New York: Crabtree, 1998.

Wilkins, Sally. *Temperate Forests.* The Bridgestone Science Library: Ecosystems. Mankato, Minn.: Bridgestone Books, 2001.

Internet Sites

Autumn Leaf Scrapbook
http://mbgnet.mobot.org/sets/temp/leaves

BBC Education Landmarks: Forests
http://www.bbc.co.uk/education/landmarks/
standard/forests

The Rainforest Workshop
http://kids.osd.wednet.edu/Marshall/
rainforest_home_page.html

Index/Word List

Word Count: 114
Early-Intervention Level: 15

Editorial Credits
Martha E. H. Rustad, editor; Kia Bielke, cover designer and illustrator;
   Kimberly Danger, photo researcher

Photo Credits
Bruce Coleman/John Daniels, 6
CORBIS, 1, 4, 16
Henryk Kaiser/eStock Photography/Picturequest, cover
John Elk III, 20
Unicorn Stock Photos/A. Gurmankin, 12
Visuals Unlimited/Norris Blake, 8; Jeff Greenberg, 10; Joe McDonald, 14;
   Ron Spomer, 18